To
Port Seton

this book w[t]
a Thankyou to John Bellany
for permission to use his
painting on the cover of Pursuit.

Gillian Bouie
20 June 2000

PURSUIT

Other poetry collections by George Bruce

Sea Talk (1944)
Selected Poems (1947)
Landscape and Figures (1967)
Collected Poems (1970)
The Red Sky (1985)
Perspectives (1987)

Scottish Contemporary Poets Series
(for further details of this series please contact Scottish Cultural Press)

James Aitchison, *Brain Scans;* 1 898218 91 9
Tom Bryan, *North East Passage;* 1 898218 57 9
Gerry Cambridge, *The Shell House;* 1 898218 34 X
Ken Cockburn, *Souvenirs and Homelands;* 1 898218 93 5
Jenni Daiches, *Mediterranean;* 1 898218 35 8
Robert Davidson, *Total Immersion;* 1 898218 95 1
Valerie Gillies, *The Ringing Rock;* 1 898218 36 6
Stanley Roger Green, *Waiting for the Mechanic;* 1 898218 94 3
William Hershaw, *The Cowdenbeath Man;* 1 898218 68 4
Brian Johnstone, *The Lizard Silence;* 1 898218 54 4
Anne MacLeod, *Standing by Thistles;* 1 898218 66 8
Angus Martin, *The Song of the Quern;* 1 898218 92 7
Ken Morrice, *Talking of Michelangelo;* 1 898218 56 0
Siùsaidh NicNèill, *All My Braided Colours;* 1 898218 55 2
Walter Perrie, *From Milady's Wood;* 1 898218 67 6
Maureen Sangster, *Out of the Urn;* 1 898218 65 X
Kenneth C Steven, *The Missing Days;* 1 898218 37 4

Also

Robert Davidson (ed), *After the Watergaw;* 1 84017 024 7
John Rice, *The Dream of Night Fishers;* 184017 025 5
Maurice Lindsay, *News of the World;* 1 898218 32 3
Maurice Lindsay, *Speaking Likenesses;* 1 898218 96 X
Douglas Kynoch, *The Ministers Cat;* 1 898218 18 8
Anne Forsyth (ed), *Canty and Couthie;* 1 898218 04 8
Ian McDonough (ed), *The Ice Horses;* 1 898218 85 4

PURSUIT

Poems
1986–1998

George Bruce

SCOTTISH CULTURAL PRESS
Edinburgh

First Published 1999 by
Scottish Cultural Press
Unit 14, Leith Walk Business Centre
130 Leith Walk
Edinburgh EH6 5DT
Tel: 0131 555 5950 • Fax: 0131 555 5018
e-mail: scp@sol.co.uk

British Library Cataloguing in Publication Data
A catalogue record for this book is available from the British Library

The publisher acknowledges support received from the Scottish Arts
Council towards the publication of this volume

THE SCOTTISH **ARTS** COUNCIL

ISBN: 1 84017 031 X

Printed and bound by
Polestar AUP Aberdeen Ltd, Aberdeen, Scotland

Dedicated to the memory
of
Elizabeth Bruce
1907–1994

In Gratitude

I record my gratitude to John Bellany for allowing me to reproduce his painting *Three Fishers* for the cover of this book (see also p. 27). I record my gratitude to Lucina Prestige for the editorial assistance including glossary, the typing of the book by Andrew Bruce, the work done on the title poem by Malcolm Mackay, and advice from Margot Rhead and Elizabeth Cumming. I acknowledge that without Maurice Lindsay's practical encouragement this book would not exist.

Acknowledgements

Poems in the collection have appeared in *Lines Review, Chapman, New Writing Scotland, Interim* (U.S.A.), *The Broken Fiddle, The Five Touns Festival Collection, Where the Land Meets the Sea, The Scottish Dog* (Aberdeen University Press), *The New Makars, Under Cover, Zed 2 0* (Akros)*, The Scotsman, Breaking New Ground, A Very Still Life* (Atelier Books).

Contents

Preface

Pursuit: Poems 1986–1998 is my latest collection of new poems and poems uncollected. One poem, *House with Back Garden*, is an exception to this statement, having been published in *Perspectives – Poems 1970–1986*. It is included on account of its being part of a sequence which developed from it, which itself is part of the autobiographical first section. This aspect of autobiography may also explain why poems in Scots, or mainly in Scots, are not given a separate section.

These poems do not occupy a separate compartment in my mind. They link the past with the present. They belong to the flow of my consciousness. To have spoken 'English' when I was with my peers when I was a boy would have been to put on airs, though I expect the majority of words were 'English' – the shared written vocabulary, but spoken differently. In 1958 Kurt Wittig commented on my poems: "His 'English' is, in its own way, quite as Scottish as any Lallans."[1] Robert Louis Stevenson commented on the Scots in his own poems: "not caring if it hailed from Lauderdale or Angus, from the Mearns or Galloway."[2] This reflected my attitude when I wrote Scots generally, but in the present collection two poems are in Aberdeenshire Scots, *On the Edge – the Broch* and *Mindin David Murison*.

In the former I respond to various situations and happenings in my childhood. The varying degrees of Scots, and the absence of Scots, reflects the changing conditions. So 'hame' is the word used when I am with my playmates on the sands, but it becomes 'home' from the moment I am in that place, though Scots was not excluded. Even so when I was out with my father it is diminished. Released from him it takes over. I did not deliberate on this matter. It is an acknowledgement of what happened. This is a matter of integrity. The poem, *Mindin David Murison*, respects the great lexicographer's origin in Fraserburgh, to which he returned for the last years of his life. For him, this was a matter of integrity.

The image of the perdurable rock, and the image of the fisherman accommodating the sea's force, so that he and his boat became one thing was a major resource to me in the late 1930s when all humane values were threatened. Such imagery provided the main impulse for my early poems. When in September 1996 I received from Tom Bryan, then Writer-in-Residence at Macduff Arts Centre, Banffshire, two photographs by Orlando Gualtieri, one of *Cliff Face Erosion*, the other of *A Beach with Sea at Night-Fall*,[3] and was asked to respond to these in poems, I replied: "I am pierced by them…They seize me and I turn from them, for they tell me of the moment of the moment that I am."

The demand was for a wider, more accommodating integrity, a wholeness which would contain opposites. This is the impulse which underpins this book. It is the motif of the poem, *Pursuit*. For Cezanne such incorporation was essential to the integrity of his last great paintings of Le Mont Sainte-Victoire. In the poem I interpret statements from Cezanne's letters:

> All noted. To each and all, he,
> the image-creator, maker, responds.
> From any given form from earth sky or water,
> he could not turn away. Accept he must.
> To reject any is to reject all,

On his last journey to the site Cezanne collapsed, and later died.

George Bruce
Edinburgh 1999

1. *The Scottish Tradition in Literature* by Kurt Wittig (Oliver and Boyd, 1958)
2. Preface to 'Poems in Scots' in *Underwoods*
3. *Where the Land Meets the Sea,* Photographs by Orlando Gualtieri. Text by north-east writers, edited by Tom Bryan

RETURN

Departure and Departure and ...

Someone is waving a white handkerchief
from the train as it pulls out with a white
plume from the station and rumbles its way
to somewhere that does not matter. But
it will pass the white sands and the broad sea
that I have watched under the sun and moon
in the stop of time in my childhood as I am
now there again and waiting for the white
handkerchief. I shall not see her again
but the waters rise and fall and the horizon
is firm. You who have not seen that line
hold the brimming sea to the round earth
cannot know this pain and sweetness of departure.

On the Edge – The Broch[1]

Dedicated to the memory of Gilbert Buchan, skipper of
The Replenish, and to his father, James

"To live here is to live on the edge,"
said James Buchan, 7½ Mid Street,
Inverallochy, skipper of *The Buchans.*
Gilbert's father, the name being common
but not the man, a'body kent him – 7½.[2]
Ithers micht near company his thochts,
but nae in winnan the exact words,
skipper Joseph Duthie and Love – his T name –
amang them, good men a', wha thocht
ayont their trade o' huntin herrin,
or through it, in hope a truth would oot,
beginning frae the facts o' life gien them.
James Buchan's life, handbreadths from the sea,
knew it put at nowt the vanities of class or cash.
Gilbert began from here; respect must be earned.
So he gives his boat an honest name, *Replenish,*
in hope through work on the sea's face she has
a proper return, though aye in doubt. The edge
aye there. Tae his loons it meant nae thing,
e'en when the sea brocht tae oor feet on the tide
a ba, we blootered aboot the sands or nichtfa
wioot a thocht, for a'thing was in its richt place –
the sea, the sands, the South Kirk spire, the links
wi room eneugh for 'the winds o' heiven', as the minister
pit it, tae blaw and howl hine awa ayont the bents,
owre sheenan fields o' corn tae Mormond Hill[3] that tell't
the boats whether or no their landfall was gweed.
Miles awa agin the dark hill the gryte[4] horse
shined oot fite, steen by steen a' fite,
laid doon een agin the tither: that big,
the horse, tae walk it roon, heid tae tail,
syne back, half wey yer belly's tellin,
"It's supper time:" and aye there, they say,
'frae time memorial'[5] or the like o' that.

4

The meen cam up and tide gaed oot
and the sands were as braid as ten
fitba pitches, and the inshore fishers
wi graips diggin the sands for sanle
for bait, and his yet at oor ba game
or they cried tae his tae help the wark.
As the sanle leapt oor hand's flasht,
but they, like lichtnin back tae their
sand hame, but again an again the graips
flung up sods o' sand and his loons catcht
the sma fish in air or they dove,
like they were siller needles richt through
thon thick sog oot o' sicht and deep doon
and never seen again. Syne we ran for hame.

Home: bed: nor-east corner: night winds beat
about the granite house. The lighthouse beam
stalks the room, is blunted on the walls,
sweeps off, and in the black dark
in sea's far-off roar, I sleep deep.
Morning – white light swims about the town.
The church spire at the top of our street
is encased in blue. The Central Public School,
encased in blue, waits for me. A white gull,
bead-eyed, sits on a lamp-post, out-stares me.
In my schoolbag is learning. It weighs one ton.

Saturday: he handed me the reins on that icy
morning at 2 Victoria Street[6] as the horse
lolloped free from Mrs McWhirter's milk delivery.
I smelt its warm leathery hide, one hand on one
big tin milk can as I stood between the two,
blowing frost like our horse, Meg, who
snorted into the air as we banged and clanged
and struck fire from the metals in the street.
Under the boards the road ran furiously
as we lifted off. Not since the chariot of the Lord
came like a whirlwind was seen such splendour

as we flew in Jim Baird's milk cart that day.
From below my grandfather's shovel beard
shouted: "Praise the Lord!" Nothing new
in that. In these days miracles
were as common as tatties and herrin'.

The first tomorrow for me began that day,
the first time my father took me, age 7 years,
to Bruce's Look-Out. It was the first time
I saw the edge. The stair in the big, dark shed,
went up and up owre a white mountain o'saut,
syne a ladder, syne a trap door, syne oot.
Blint wi licht the cauld sun brak on my heid,
and me tellt: "Scan the horizon." (I had nae mind
o' meetin that word afore. Nae doot it's in the school bag.)
It was seven in the morning: "What do you see?
Look to the horizon. See how it runs near round us.
Look east, now nor-nor east". And I saw nothing
but the sea. Then I saw the endless dark line
drawn by God that separates sea from sky.
"Look again," he said, and I saw come up
from the drowned world under the sea a mast,
a funnel, a boat. "I see a boat!" "Low
or high on the water?" I couldna tell, then
ithers cam. Syne I saw first one low on the watter,
then anither and anither. Come time clouds of gulls
were about each boat. All this I said to my father.
And he said: "Right we'll go." And sic a girnin',
an yammerin an chantin, "forty bob, forty, forty,
fifty bob, fifty, fifty, fifty," sic a barkin
an' growlin' like dogs owre meat, deaved my lugs,
in the mart that I was deef as deef Burke
the boxer. It was heiven tae get oot an smell
the tar and ile an saut at the pier heid ootbye.
Come nicht an me in bed, and the herrin quines
yet at the guttin and me hearing the sweetest
soonds ever sangs made as thae heilan deems sang
wi words I kent nae o'. I hearkened or I was asleep.

"Ye're a grander," glowered the fisher loon
at me and I glowered back. I niver thocht
ither than the Broch loon I wis like ither loons.
'The rocket's up.' Bang, bang it gaed and his
at squeel and a'body doon the streets gan gyte
tae mak the herbour. Force 9 gale and a boat
in trouble, and afore we're there the lifeboat's awa.
But na, the lifeboat's at the herbour mou witin,
hidin' in ahint the lea o' the north breakwater,
and we kent in the open sea it would be a deathboat.
So it wited and a' the folk wited, and I cam up on
the fisher loon, and his thegither threided the crood
on the Sooth Pier, and at the heid o't,
(faur eence I had catcht a conger eel)
we grippit a chine at the wa, or we'd
been blawn awa tae kingdom come. And mair
and mair folk gaithert. By the mart, hauden close,
weemen frae the Deep Sea Fishermen's Mission,
at the ready wi blankets, hot tea, dry claes
for them near droont by the watter, and at haund
an ambulance, and fishermen by the boats tethered,
but aye creakin and groanin, for there
was nae stoppin the pouer o' that watter.
The hail toon wis there, a'body
frae granders in Strichen Road to Puddlestinkers –
a' them maistly eeseless folk, Curran Bun Chalmers,
(Champion Prize Winner, Black Bun Competition,
      London, England)
Butcher Macfarlane, Macdonald the Grocer, and oor
school teacher, and a hantle ithers – but a' witin,
quaet, and naething tae see but watter –
heich hills o't thrashin ootside the herbour mou,
lumps o' watter loupin the breakwater and ower
the tap o' the herbour beacon that ends the steen wa.
And his! – we're starin oor een oot stracht
afore's – sometimes nae sky, jist black watter.
Stare we micht hopin for sicht o' somethin
that meth be boat, but naething. Then sudden

she's there. Sudden she's gone aneath a wall o' watter,
and again she's there, that near I saw the FR
on her, then gone. This time nae come back,
finished, I thocht, but na, she's heich
on tap o' a wave that maun carry her stracht on,
aye and be smashed tae bits on the beacon wa.
The skipper steers her clear o't and noo
she's richt in mid-channel. We haud oor braeth –
a'body, and the lifeboat settles a meenit atween
beacon and pier, but nae eese, the cross-wave
cacht the *Golden Harvest* – say I thocht her name –
and swept awa oor hope. Still we wited, still
stared across the watters gettin dark.
And she was there further oot, syne doon, syne
up again, syne ae moment at the herbour mou,
her bow pints stracht at his, at the Sooth Pier heid!
The skipper kent a' thing, kent the shore wave's
back-wash and, bidin his time, kent it, and drove
the boatie through: and a' the folk cheerin
and greetin and dancin, and haudin een till
anither wioot a thocht, wioot a care if he
was Puddlestinker or e'en cam fae Peterheid.

"Not in the storm but in a calm night
and the stars shining down; the vast expanse
of waters, throws his thought back on fishermen.
He is in another world separated and isolated.
To live here is to live on the edge."[7]

House With Back Garden

Our granite house
by the sea – never
out of its roaring or
shushing or hacking cough –
stood steady as any rock.

A good house with good people
in it; who looked after it,
and us. Everything there
was in its right place,
except us boys, of course,
though we knew where
we ought to be.

The way to the back green
was through the big trellised
gate. It wobbled open
when pushed or kicked
which we did. We would

rush into the back garden
to kick a ball on my Dad's
lawn, a whole football team
of us. We kicked it to pieces.
Father watched us kick his
green grass to pieces,
which he had watered
and cut, and got just right.

He did not stop our game,
just watched from the window.
I went into the house. He said:
"My poor lawn." I cried. He said:
"Never mind, you enjoyed yourselves."
And then laughed. No grudge.
He patted me on the head.

The Face

In the dark narrow hall-way of Father and Mother
on the mahogany table, a silver salver;
on it, etched, a woman with hair streaming
in the wind, where was no wind. The date is 1917.
My cousin Alister has returned from the trenches.

His glengarry is on the silver salver.
I see his khaki puttees tight about his legs.
He speaks in a deep voice. No-one else speaks.
No-one else has the right to speak
While the soldier from the trenches speaks.

Are there legs inside the khaki bandages?
His eyes shine a little with grey lights.
He has a moustache. His gun had a bayonet.
I have a dagger like a bayonet.

I press the bayonet against my chest.
The blade disappears but there is no blood.
Perhaps the soldier's bayonet is like that.
This war is a silent picture that is still.

It is all in the *London Illustrated News*.
Page by page the soldiers stand to attention
for ever. The generals are on horse-back.
They never move. In the silver salver
I see the face of a child. It weeps.

Father and the Silver Salver

As was his custom at
approx. 9 a.m. he returned
from the yard for coffee,

would plant his cap on the
silver salver on the hall table
and announce he was home.

He'd been on the go from
6 a.m. to yard, office, harbour.
He brought into the house

salt airs, left on the door-mat
sequins of herring scales
that flashed in sunlight.

On this fine morning the cap
did not leave the hand.
No salver. He minded

he'd met a couple, man
pushing a two-wheeled,
flat-topped float, wife

walking alongside with shut face.
On top a pile of rags, clothing,
mebbe all their worldly goods.

Down Victoria Street he went.
No sighting. The way south,
Saltoun Place, out of town,

he overtook them, paced them,
the while one hand lifting
the rags, slipping from them

the silver salver. No word spoken.
They went their way, he his.

Cliff Face Erosion

in response to the photograph by Orlando Gualtieri

'e cosi esisti' – Montale
for my brother Robert – il miglior linguista

Fae that blin mappa mundi face;
scartit, I wud look awa bit that
tae its lang daith ma face
is bondit, an will-na win awa.

I am old, yet the breathing intimacies
of air, those inspirations from the forever
fresh wildernesses of sea, even the sea pink
I picked from the marram grass as child,
has carried through the years unfearful,
trusting, secured through time into this now,
this moment of putting pen to paper as if
this wholeness, indestructible, outdated
time and gave us a permanence of being.
You tell me what I would not know.
From the frail page you stare at me
with the authority of millions of years,
and I am diminished to a point not
to be picked out even by that
electronic scan that determines existences
light years from this planet; and you
present indifferently substance and
ephemera, darknesses and lights, yet
no more are you the bastion that you were,
resisting and denying access to sea's force,
the great wave falling from you, and you
remained yourself. Now to the gnawing salt,
the flux of waters, cross-fire of elements
you concede. Ravaged, penetrated, scuffed,
deep-graven – your face is witness,
as is the human face, to the years.
I look upon your face and it is mine.
I look upon you and marvel.

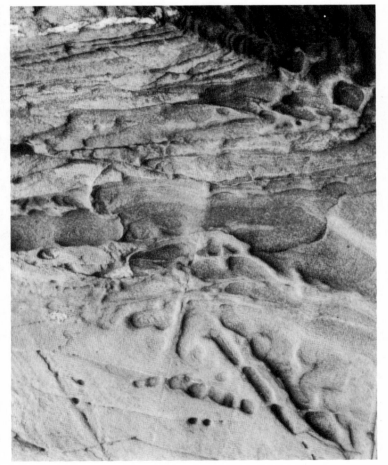

Rock erosion, small cove near Sandend   Orlando Gualtieri

Night-Fall

Nae soun: nae sea soun,
Fit wye nae sea soun?
Hid the deid-chack knockit
i the nicht an a the toun
slipt intae the lang sleep?
Me, a bairn, wakt, an nae peep
o licht fur nae sea soun sang.

Most times the shore and the sea
is telling us little enough, food
for one, another in the summer,
even in our cold North, a place
for mothers in creaking deck chairs,
children clattering their tin pails
waiting for sand-pies or little fish.
But once as night fell he was there,
the tide "that far oot – an nae soun –
cud it iver come back? an black rocks
niver seen afore, an I maun be there.
I slipt ma haun intae the cald watter
aneath the black wrack, an feel ma wye
intae the crack on the rock, an there
wis a gryte partan. Ma fingers traivelt
on an on on the shall. It wint on foriver.
Niver wis sic a crab. Feart I ran
for hame. The braith gaed oot o me.
I stopt, an took a keek back."

Dark fell on sands and rock,
but the waters were bright holding
light to themselves. The sea
had ceased its terrible proclamations.
It was as if it had yielded its powers
to another order, one hardly guessed at,
nor to be seen from our disturbed universe,
yet now some thought that they had glimpsed
that long-sought peace that lay beyond our hopes.

The Herbour Wa, MacDuff

for George Gunn

The wa! – the face o blunt rebuttal –
sea's girn, yelloch, yammer, snash, greet
an then thunner that wud smore a – this
the wa took on, whiles the squat beacon licht
signalled hope fae its steen stack tae boats
storm-driven, that, but for it, meth stravaig
heid-on tae wa, an that's an en o't,
an them aboard. Exac timin, steady hauns, keen ee,
tae haud her deid-mid the run o watter tween piers.
The Provider, wi a wecht o haddock, cod, ling, sole,
twa monkfish an a conger we cud duin wioot,
netted saxty mile nor-nor-east Kinnaird,
the nor wun at her stern, heids in atween the gap,
nae a thocht, nae a doot at the rin-in, driven
bi thon hard race. They're for hame, diesel pooer,
as the boats, steam an sail, through a the years.

Mist

Mist shrouds the Firth,
contains all, allows entry
only to the finger
of the mind, contains
time past, hard-backs
resistant to wear of water,
predators predating all
kind, or simples, uni-cellular
expressions, or us mulched to
such fineness as that transparent
air in stratosphere provides.

Moss Agate

As if the North green-weedy sea
had entered in and met the South,
unctuous and vinous, suffusing reds
with subtle lights of plum.

And this is stone and common.
No moonstone omen from eternity
but sea-washed, bound for Scotland
when the cosmic pot was on the boil.

Something between the soft, wild lights
of a winter sky and any careless
autumn afterthought, now transfixed,
like Leonardo's famous smile.

Haiku for John Ferguson,
Rector of Fraserburgh Academy

Coming home
to the sea-town
shared interests
much understanding

The sun leans
on the low landscape
the sea is kindly
affection stirs

The flat stone
in Kirkton Kirkyard
by the sea's mouth
spells our endless end

Ian in the Broch

To Ian McNab, civil engineer and singer, who sang the
Iona *Gloria* in St Giles' Cathedral, Edinburgh, at a
commemoration of the 1400th anniversary of the death of
Saint Columba, memorably

Returned, but never away.
Rain storms at arrival, but
sun prevails. Brightness is all,
white on the wings of the glancing
fulmar. Wave breaks, white light
shakes from its blue. All one
to him at the centre, an internet
in himself: hardly a step
at the harbour, and another
McNab has a word with him.
This is the flower of friendships
engendered in the generations,
caught up now in this talk-talking
town, aye, toun, 'fou's aa?'
'fit's deein?', and on again
as if heaven were not about him
in this place in time, where
the running boy runs forever
in the mind, yet he would know,
know his place, know how
the lighthouse light projects its beam,
timely, exact on the dark waters.
But look at the tapered rollers
bearing the great weight of the
gyrating mirrors, steel supports,
that issue the light to all seamen.
Now he walks the town simply
as if the common talk's enough,
but from him, from head and lips –
GLORIA!

FOLK

Responsibilities

for Stephen Strachan

The little boy with the little drum
gave it the exact tap.
"I tap it and tap it,"
said the boy unsmiling
for the responsibility was great.

If the rat-tat-tat had not been
exact
on time
all
was lost.

He stood alone
before
the eight players of
Pencaitland Primary School Jazz Band.

The face of the boy listened
to the silences between
the beats.
When
all ended and the applause
broke the bonds of the band
he heard nothing of it.

His eyes stared in wonder
as his heart beat out
the exact
tap tap.

Invocation

o a thae gaitherins i the High Street an Canongate betokinin the Scottish Poetry Library

Wha cud hae thocht that I
trimmlin on the lip o time,
ma licht at peep, cud yet
staun here an harken
the multitude murmurs risin
an fain at derk frae closes,
vennels, howfs, dens o sin,
the like that poet chiels hae haunted
owre a the years – an noo a gaithered
here ablow. Aince Scott, the boy, his mou
ticht shut, in Sibbald's libr'ry, gawpt
at yon chiel, Burns, nor daurd
say words. This was a true respec:
while doun the Canongate the bard
himsel peyed oot his hard won
puns in stane to honour Fergusson,
an yet a third jined in, Stevenson.
Een a fourth in oor time
stude at the grave, Garioch.
The auld toun gied them drink
an words, an sangs, an hellish deeds.
Sae as we stap oot this nicht
think nocht o the flim-flam-fleerie
lichts, that ken nocht o this
maist wanchancy past, that's
in us noo: as we bide here
at *The Warld's En* maun harken
til anither soun an lat thae
whisperin delicates, the lang thochts,
the breathin o the spirit o
Tessa's[1] rare "Medusa" sang.
Tak tent, harken, an let
the new quaet voice be here.

The Flat
Scottish Poetry Library

21

Epistle 1: To Edwin Morgan

A response to Edwin Morgan's invitation to submit a poem
for publication in *New Writing, Scotland*, which he and Carl
MacDougall edited

Your letter, the best thing
that happened for a time, since I
am at odds with my self, and it
brought me momentarily together.
BUT doubt steps in between
the pen and paper as to whether
any good cd come from a body
too young for my age.

                              It's a
pleasure to be with you now as I am,
to see your smile in my mind
as I do now, and to pride my
self that I might have some thing
still to bring out my oddity.

No more journeys; and when I
am thinking back to the last
N.C., U.S.A. affray, I cannot
stay my eye on the blue butterfly,
handsbreadth winged on the red
azaleas by the campus lakeside:
it takes off for habitation
for blacks, which I, misguided
surprised, find at a dead end
where the road turns to dirt track
running by the railline (freight
only.) I shd have been on tother side
happy with whites in their forever cars.
STILL I had a southern breakfast
(7.30 – 10.30 a.m.) with Mary de Rachewiltz,[1]
E.P.'s daughter on a quiet Spring day
in a colonial, one-storey, white pillared

home (as the Americans would say.) Sat
in the portico, with terra cotta colour
steps, flanked by two Romanesque urns,
white. Cool. She wore a pale green dress.
Beyond the garden, azaleas and shrubs in it,
nothing, rough grass, weeds. A tornado had
taken away the firestation outbye
and all the other buildings, so
there we were in a nothing.
'What thou lovest well remains
          the rest is dross'
the motto for her *Discretions*.
Was she mistaken to pour out
her love on Babbo? Still does as she
annotates the *Cantos*. I say Joseph Macleod.
'Joseph Gordon Macleod wrote *The Ecliptic*,'
she quotes the line from the *Cantos*,
'And I know nothing of him.' I oblige,
remark we were to visit Pound. Venice.
All arranged. Pound ill. 'He came back
to Brunnenburg.' No more spoken till.
'Come to Brunnenburg.' I tremble
at the thought of that high Schloss
with suffering Pound and his women;
have enough ado keeping my own
ghosts under the floor. This house
creaks with them. Yours, affec. G.B.

Epistle 2: Response to Invitation to Meet a Memory

On 24 September 1989, from 2–4 p.m., in Alderston Auditorium, Kansas Union, we will remember Professor Edward L. Ruhe, who died on 29 June 1989. Please join us for this memorial service and for the reception to follow.

Department of English, University of Kansas,
to George Bruce, Edinburgh, Scotland.

May 1982, met him, and then only thrice or so,
nor ever after. He was at the table next to us,
Fellows Dining hall, National University, Canberra.
Alone, uneasily he smiled; unprompted introduced himself
as: "Ruhe – commonest name in German cemeteries – Peace."
The humour was not lost when unpeaceably he drove
round roundabouts along straightways on the wrong
side of the road. We survived lorries, cars, long-vehicles,
while he talked, talked of "the burial customs of aboriginals,"
switching on a bend of the road to "Smart – Christopher
Smart of *Song to David* fame, but *"Jubilate Agno!"*
As he turns his head he gives out the line:
"For the mouse is a creature of great personal valour."
The voice holds on course. He is the professor in essence,
enquirer and admirer of the inhabitants of the planet,
forever strange to him, yet kin.

                       Afterwards I looked at
the kangaroo, the guana, galah, pelican, lyre-bird,
and saw how peculiar were the brown sparrows
fluttering in the dust at my Scottish door-step.

Epistle 3: To Maurice and Joyce Lindsay

To hansel their new home on Milton Hill

The ghosts of your homes wander through
my address books. The aches of iron trams,
juddering and squealing through Hillhead,
founder on your step at Athole Gardens.
Elegant Southpark Avenue fades into night.
At Gartocharn dogs howl, children tumble,
horses nose your doors, the loch stays
at a distance; the broad parks of Annan –
gone. I remember a red gown, a girl
in misty St Andrews, who had, she said,
"a friend called Maurice Lindsay."
Before the unchanging features of friendship
the irritations of the silly world
vanish. Now stand solitary on the hill
as the tides run silently below;
each moment holds our being – this know.

Epistle 4: To Ruby (5), Holly (3), Shirley and Timothy Cumming

Written on a Christmas Card reproducing *Hunters in the Snow* by Bruegel the Elder

Just as it was when Icarus fell
out of the sky, as Peter Bruegel saw it,
the great adventure ending miserably,
no-one paid any attention – the ploughman
went on ploughing, the shepherd shepherding,
the fisherman fishing, the ship puffing
its sails for somewhere else, so it is
with *Hunters in the Snow*. They pass
the women warming at the fire, who give no heed;
a cart with provender heads for the village;
a woman, back bent with a load of faggots
is crossing a bridge, snow crowned, earth
bound in whiteness, sky beams back
the winter message. Her heart is on
the dry stick blaze in the hearth of home.
It is the play upon the ice for old
and young that holds each to their moment,
as the bird of prey holds to the sky
forever there in the miraculous landscape.
No-one looks up, all are busy being
themselves. Good people, all!
Be yourselves, and time will stop
for you in the dance of Holly and Ruby.

Epistle 5: A Thank-You to John Bellany

for his card (Christmas 1997), especially for the painting of three
fishermen standing on the deck of their boat

Their trade's to trawl the seas,
hunt fish, gut fish, land fish –
no sweet job, so some will
to God in heaven, some to booze
to keep them 'richt for the morn'
to face wind and water and doubt.
So they contain the rough deal
of life they've got, make it
look easy – 'that's the wey it is,'
but, John, you plant the three
fronting us from the deck, and one
half-hidden in the hold's dark,
who've tholed the cauld of day
and night since Noah's flood.
The big bag-net spewed out
the mixter-maxter o a kinds,
spattered the boards with blood;
oilskins, gum-boots, hands, fingers
flecked with blood. No silver darlings
now, no red-spotted plaice now, no
fluke soft-gliding on the sand, no
flashing ling, no staring cod, no
glittering shoals o a thae peerie fish
that soom in perfect harmony thegither.
Job done. Each, straight upright, strains
to be man, carrying the weight
of the wealth of the prodigality
of sea. They prepare a table,
offering it to us for squander.
One, mouth agape, a silent agony,
another, arms rigid, fingers clutch,
but at the centre of the trinity,
the Christ-man with the three-pointed fish,
the skate. He clamps it to his body.
They are in judgement, but judge.
The betrayal is ours.

Soup and Sherry

It was 3.30 in the afternoon, mid-November
and I was calling on Bill Gillies.
(Sir William Gillies, R.S.A., R.A. etcetera.)
"Come in," he says, "We'll have soup.
You won't be drinking and driving
so we'll have sherry." Didn't like
the idea of the combination, but
the lentil soup was hottering
on the stove so there was nothing for it
but swallow it with the sherry.
There was a painting on the easel
of Temple, the village where we were.
It didn't look like the rainy street
off which I'd just come. In it
the moon was up and silvering
the length of it, pavement, tarmac road,
squat houses, and touching up
two black trees, winter trees,
but each twig starting from its branch
as if Spring were in it. I looked out
the window. Nothing like the painting.
No glimmering windows along the street.
He was stirring the soup. He didn't look up.
"I catched a painting last night."
I could see him casting on the Esks,
North Esk, South Esk, Leithen Water, Falla.
How many paintings got away? "Soup's ready."
How many poems slip back into my dark sea?

Gillies

Self-portrait. 1941. Oil on canvas. 86 by 70cm. Scottish National
Gallery of Modern Art

Did he know as he put the self on canvas
that stood there merely holding the brushes,
looking from there back at the stranger,
the light was upon him and about him;
about him light touched by enlightenment,
the painting claiming the silence,
creating that to which the final word aspires?

Mindin David Murison

"It's nae mows," he said tae me
fin' I hid tell't him that a bodie
wis jist 'kenspeckle' an he hid said,
"Na, ill teenit" o the man fa made
a monkey o wir tongue. Aye, bit said
wi twinklin ee. Sae I mind
this humorous chiel, thrawn till's daith,
niver gien tae bleat aboot his sel,
bit coorse on aa that stuid atween him
an the grite en o cheivin the last wurd
i the buik o Scots. Syne he wud be
king o aa, his heid repository
o territory that raxed fae Picts tae present,
fae John o Groats tae Tweed.
Sic a wecht o warlds tae cairry,
an that he did maist lichtly.
That deen hame, tween roarin seas
an Mormond Hill. Bit niver feenished.
He tripped alang, sma-boukit man,
gryte hertit, mair than ony meth unnerstan.

At Mayakovsky's Statue

Ae shouder heisted
tae ca doun
the deid warld o offices –
Konfer, Konfer, Konfer!

It's nae as easy as that.

So he sticks oot a chin –
he'll tak the warld on't:
bit that glower kens
it's nae that easy
to be
'a clood in breeks'.

He wud mairch
oot o's orra duds
stracht intae history.

By God, he did:
noo stauns a stane man
at this Moscow corner,
Mayakovsky Square.

Peace

Pairty at a Collective Tea Fairm, Georgia 1973

The Russian Orthodox Christian Georgian Communist,
Member o the Supreme Soviet,
cheerman o the pairty
heistit his glass
tae me.

Uttered.

Forty Baptist Kirk Georgian Communist basses
heistit their glasses.

Uttered.

I ken nae Georgian.

At the stert o the feast
twenty-twa bottles stude on the table.
At the hinner-end o't
thirty-twa stude.

Then I kent a'.
Noo I ken nae Georgian.

The Crescent

In memory of Martin Prestige at 4 Warriston Crescent (1935–1979)

[Martin Calder Prestige: "His death, at the early age of 44, removes from the world of developmental neurobiology one of its most incisive minds and able investigators." *Nature* 29 Nov. 1979]

This is a place called home –
home because we live here
looking at the park where girls
crack their hockey-sticks together
and boys play football furiously

because the Water of Leith at
our back door at a moment's notice
blows itself up and runs off in fine
fettle with ducks, pianos and any old
iron, then deflates to the burn it is

because conversation interrupts
shopping expeditions we know
people this way. Suddenly one
is no longer there and we are not
what we were. This one now

whose slight form moving with
difficulty looked in for a few years,
slipped into several minds and hearts.
We, as usual, thought nothing of this
till suddenly his attentive ear,

his glance, interested, through the shining
windows of his glasses, was no longer
present. There was an impression of
serenity – it stretched from him
all the way to 33.[1] People smiled

and didn't know why. He honoured us
with his suffering, never shown.
Now there remains the slight space of
his awkward walk which cannot quite
be filled.

Elizabeth in the Garden

"It is," she said, "a windflower,[1] Japanese."
The white windflower at the wall is still.
We sit in the moment as if we'd
stepped outside the running world
and made a here-and-now that stopped
the ripened apple's drop to earth,
caught in that round moment that sought
a word, yet dared not say for
on my mortal breath the word would
perish. Would God that this, this word,
the Word would spread its timeless time,
but that Rwanda's cries and all its kind
here and about, proclaim the self-destructive mind.

Words for Jenni, 8 July 1996

A pendant for my granddaughter visiting Thailand while I was at
Lake Maggiore

That day the lake was silver, hardly
an airy whisper about and you
were in the company of Buddha.
Perhaps his serenity discovered you.
So it was here as the chemistry of heaven
suffused the waters with a thousand colours.
This day may the beatitude be yours.

Castle Tioram, Loch Moidart

The tide comes in and empties the castle
of all but its bloody memories. The tourists
are gone, the last bustling to the shore
before the tide cut-off, leaving their litter.
Paper bags spin up draughty holes and out,
whisked out to sea. Lords of the Isles
lived here, thinking to themselves – forever.
Gone. What human kind were they anyway?
Pride, courage, cruelty in them, no doubt.
Evening – the loch stills. In its shimmer
Tioram trembles. From the dark cube laughter,
echoes of children, the new invaders –
Andrew, Ken, Karen, Jennifer, Ben –
a play pen for them. Night,
skraichs – the sea birds have it for themselves.

In the Train

"Are you going to Glasgow?" he said,
as only a man from Glasgow could say.
There was nowhere else for this train to go
so I said nothing. Neither "yes" or "no",
but stared at the gray man in gray, gray hair,
gray face, his chin and his nose so close,
as if no teeth between, his eyes shut tight,
his lips drawn tight to let nothing get in.
Then as the train sped on its way the light
broke new, spreading its beams on fields
of stubble and green on this November day,
but all I saw was a faceless man,
thin flesh a cover for bones. Till Glasgow came.
He opened gray eyes, and bright they shone. "Glasgow!"
he bawled with a laugh that shoved off wrong,
and Sauchiehall Street was one long song.

"I come from Shetland."
Time melts as if before acetylene's force.
Eyes open on micaceous beach.
Tides at a race strand
a whale. Skies high with light,
with birds harsh in chorus strew
the air – talk, talking of gulls,
terns, guillemots, puffins and petrels.
Beneath – the provident seas that
would sustain multitude, but that
we came.

At Lake Maggiore

5 a.m. 28 June 1996, Hotel du Parc, Stresa

Oggi aurora con dita rosa.
Dove, dove gli strumenti alati
di celebrazione felicita?

This day 'the rosy-fingered dawn.'
Where, where are the winged
instruments of celebration?

Vibrations

'Be nocht hoity-toity'

You'll mind on the gran tenor
wha's tap note brak the gless
on the table-tap intae twa thoosand pieces.
You'll mind on 'the classic case'
o the wa's o Jericho.
And then there wis the hen
that look't Mrs McPhee
straucht in the ee,
an she split.

Noo abody has their vibrations,
witin in the back-shop
or unner the bed
or spewed oot sudden
frae a shiny computer.

So, watch yer step this fine mornin,
my mannie.

PURSUIT

Weys o Self-Preservin Natur

We socht for bait on the bay sands, braid
ahint the far-oot sea, whiles at nicht-fa
and the mune up. As the sanle leapt
oor haunds flasht, and they like lichtnin
back to their sand hame, but agen and agen
the graips threw up sods o sand
and his loons cacht the sma fish in the air
or they dove, like they were siller needles,
richt through thon thick sog oot o sicht
and deep doon and never seen agen,
and we thocht naething o't.

We socht for safticks for bait, green backs
noo slippit oot their hard shalls that floatit
in the shallow pools whaur the flukes bided
on the sand, *that* like the sand that nae ee
kent ane frae tither, til lang staunin cauld
in the watter a ripple kittled the sole
o my fit and I cacht her and pit her in my pail
and saw the speckles on her like sand
and teemed her back and saw her soom awa,
and we thocht naething o't.

Yestreen oor telly took's tae keek aneath
the watters o Chesapeake Bay to goggle at
a monster screen-size crab witin on's love
but she scrawled by him on the sand
and oot the frame, syne in agen and oot
the tither side, and in agen as she were
blin tae him and what he's aifter. Sudden
his preen-heid een on stalks stare oot.
Sudden he hauds her tae him in's iron airms:
syne naething: nae muve. For twa lang days
she's in the jile: syne her carapace, jist that,
heists itsel aff her body, sae it seems, floats free
yet agen they're rock-still till she, gentle
– and delicate in her saft skin – turns ower

aneath her man; and he nae monster noo,
his grip lat go, wites, respectfu o his dame,
or frae her sel soom up thae eggs
that mak himsel tae spew oot the milk
tae fertilize, ensure the continuity
o the tribe Brachyura: this the climax
o their ploy, they unkennin that I and millions
geck, and whiles I watch, my guid-wife puts
into this auld haund a clam-shall fossil
brocht tae Edinburgh frae Chesapeake Bay,
one hunder and fifty million years auld.
Aince there stirred under this shall – life.
I thocht o the bearers o the chyne o life
that would gang on and on or lang deid this haund,
and yet the mair I vrocht at thocht
the mair I kent hoo peerie was the thocht.

Blin boozed-up his faither struck him
time and time agen, and he was oot the door.
He struck oot sooth. The lift gaed the wrang wey,
turned aff tae a side-road, syne intae a sma glen.
He slept in the lea o a stane dyke, a burn ran by.
Mornin. The mist was risen afore him, mixed in
wi the floorish o gean and blackthorn: bird sang,
teuchats flapped aboot the derk plooed fields,
lambs bleat frae the green field tither side.
He gaed nae heed: he's on his way tae the A68.
She tell't him the A68's for lifts. Noo
in Lon'on toun she's in the moneys there,
and her wi freens. 'Mither o God!' she said,
tae her pimp, 'I'll no dae that.' And him,
'Christ then ye're for't. I'v dune wi you.'
Hoo mony gang their weys tae the gowden city?
He fund his wey til't a'richt. A wrang!
Whaur, whaur his hame, his shall o comfort,
his ingan residence o love? There by the staney banks,
Sweet Thames run softly til I end my song,[1]
he bides aneath the airches o Westminster Brig.

Up-by the Palace o Westminster, Mither o Parliaments,
and mither at the tap eidently protectin her brood
frae the storms o divisions in retour for lealty,
as we ken noo, seein their doups jig up and doon
frae green upholstery, theirsels upholstered weel eneuch,
makin just laws preservin them that his and them
that hisna as they are, but mair-so the noo.
This their naitral hame, if no quite that, the place
where maist they ken themsels, at the hert o Lon'on toun.
London, *Sovereign of cities, semeliest in sight.*
Above all ryvers thy Ryver hath renowne,
Whose beryall stremys, pleasaunt and preclare,
Where many a swanne doth swymme with wyngis fare.
Upon thy lusty Brigge of pylers white
Been merchauntis full royall to behold.[2]
And upon heich the pillars o Society: plc,
wha haud the cairts, them a', and unnerneath discairds,
members o the Free Air Sociability Society,
unlimited – free stinks, free quarters, ludgins
shared by a' creepin things – winos, wide-boys,
crack addicts, chancers wha didna tak their chance,
traivellers wha's traivellin's ended, a deein man
wi a dog, a lassie wi a bairnie at her breist –
and him, nae prodigal, but pit-oot: his nicht-hoose,
dwallin place, a shauchle o caird-board boxes.
A stound o pitie gaed tae the hert,[3] quo Lorimer.
For him was nae retour, nae forgien faither,
nae hame in the black hole o angst whaur
bided his progenitors; they wha catapulted him
intae this life or daith or mixter-maxter o the baith.
'Faither, forgie them, for they kenna what they dae'
The crab, the clam, the sanle, fluke unkennan ken.

The Chair
Poet's and Painter's

chair – a seat for one person
Oxford English Dictionary
cheer, chear, cheir-chair
Concise Scots Dictionary
kathedra – a seat
Greek–English Lexicon

Greek gives the chair dignity, suggests cathedral,
a bishop's seat, hieratic, 'dim religious light', but
'Poets's Chair?' No! Na! in Scots 'Makar's Cheer',
frae whilk the makar Robert Henryson began the
anely great, tragic makar's tale in Lallan tongue.
The Testament of Cresseld, screivin in winter.
    "I mend the fire and beikit me about
    Then tuik ane drink my spreitis to comfort
    And armit me weill fra the cauld thair out."

Sic a cheer for guid Maister Henryson, teacher,
maun sober be as fits the man, durable, siccar
as the aik frae whilk it cam, its seat comfortable
whaur a man meth set his doup lang hours,
legs nae funcy, at joints tenon to mortise firm,
airms fluent in style, supportive, convenient
for the poet while deep in thocht, or drappin aff,

or in a dwaum seekin solace frae warldly cares,
afore the neist blast o words, thunderin his lugs,
comes roarin tae his pen. Sic a cheer had I
and thocht the seasoned wuid would last for aye.
Syne agin a' natur it cam to be anither *thing*.

Wife   It couldna be but him that knocked the cheer
tae kingdom come. Nae meenit still
but raxed himsel, one wey an tither,
forard an back, his pen in's nieve,
warslin wi yon cheer, tormentin't, daein
a fandango on the flair, stumpin aroon
the room huntin ae word, a ithers bein wrang,
syne pechin at the desk, heid bowed doon,
he thinks he's cacht it in his haund,
he's balanced on twa legs, the hinder twa in air,
the puir thing strivin tae haud thegither,
taigelt wi his sinews, wrigglin tae get awa.
Sudden he pu's the cheer aneath his bum,
he thinks he's got the measure, the richt beat
o the words: now they'll sing for him, groan,
moan, smile, lauch for him: he's happy,
awa wi't – ower the mune, gone tae
a dear green place (he says) whaur peace
breathes ower a, leavin ahint in sair travail
the cheer that's taen frae him his fevered fears.

Poet   Na, na. I sat me doon on't fine and cosy
cocked an ee at my braw time-piece –
snoozing time for me in my auld cheer
that cam tae me from my good business father,
a man o sense, who had nae time
for flim-flam poesie but 'held straight on
for deals.' He was 'well thought of,' respected,
wearin a black top-hat at funerals. Syne
in mid-thocht I'm gruppit frae ahint,
roon my middle and ablow – a randy customer
wha, octopus-like, flings its airms

there's mair than twa, aboot my breist,
twines its legs roond mine – I'm in
a straight jacket – bangs my heid
shoves it tae this white paper on the desk,
and in my lugs words o the cheer commence:
"Sgriobh! Scrieve! Write!" – the command
in a' three leeds, the ancient tongue, Gaelic,
language of the Garden of Eden, (the Gaels say,)
the Lallan tongue, my ain, aince the King's Scots.
English as spoken here in Scotland: but scrieve what?
Whispers, whispers, "la chaise du peinture,"
The Yellow Chair, Vincent's chair.

In Arles that Spring the lark rose
from the cornfield to sing for him.
Skies rejoiced, sang their blue for him.
The petals of the orchard showered about him,
each blossoming on the knife, the brush,
in the chemistry of paint. In Arles
from dawn to dusk the sun shone for him.
He painted the yellow sun. He painted
the sower as the sun drove earthwards
and the hand of the sower was the hand
of the god of creation. He painted
the sway in the corn as the organic
earth-force ordered him. The vault
made its statement, no words for such utterance.
The charge set, the fuse lit, earth leapt,
the onrush in a gyre spiralled the cypresses.
Skies hurried their thunders in oes and whorls,
hurtled him. In his wonderment he became
them. No respite. The eyes of the stars were his,
entered him, force unleashed, leashed,
channelled to brain, hand, encounter
with canvas – all to be rejoiced in. No:
such unfair advantage – a universe expounding
its force, had done so in quake, volcano,
earth-crust opening, basalt flow, rock,

47

through geological time, now a concentrate
in him, demanding him to contain such violences,
trap all in the small rectangle. There was
blood at his listening ear, blood at his eyes.
His astounded look was in the black cloud of crows
darkening its yellow: but about and about the town
bright undulating meadows, a yellow sea – buttercups,
"I shall paint my little house yellow. I want it
to be the house of light for everyone.
Let the sun walk into my house."
The sunflowers spoke to him:
'L'oeil du soleil, c'est l'oeil de Dieu.'
I shall put them on the walls of my room.
He put twenty burning suns in the atelier
for glory: their hosannas possessed him,
but in the bedroom "square deal furniture,
the wooden beds are like fresh butter."
Two chairs had their beginnings in a tree
nearby and in the grasses of the field,
products of the slow labour of country people.
He stared at the chair where Gaugin had sat,
looked long at it where Gaugin had left
his pipe and ash on it. He'd painted the chair;
now he painted a picture of it:
"a wooden straw-covered chair yellow
all over standing on red tiles against a wall."
Planted now by the painter's hand,
firm, sturdy, settled, no grace
but authority, seen with the eye
of imagination and love, it proposes
no time past, no future, but is.

Pursuit

Dedicated to Elizabeth Cumming who made possible the poem by her gift, *Letters on Cézanne* by Rainer Maria Rilke

The incarnation of the world *as a thing carrying conviction*, the portrayal of a reality become imperishable through his experiencing of the object – this appeared the purpose of his inmost labours. ... and was once more on his road ... beyond the studio to a valley, ... in front of which soared the mountain range of Saint Victoire.

> *Rilke on Cézanne*,
> in a letter to Clara Rilke. Paris, 9 October 1907

Surely all art is the result of one's having been in danger, of having gone through an experience all the way to the end where no one can go any further.

> *Letter from Rilke to Clara Rilke.*
> Paris, 24 June 1907

Search, he must, in words, by words,
through words, yet never the Word.
None possessed that, could not, for
the act of possessing was itself
stained, yet one move towards
that point of certainty might be
made, but not through the verisimilitude
of changing, growing, dying nature.
As Virgil, as guide, to Dante,
so Cézanne to Rilke. Verisimilitude
gives, yields nothing, but seek
with the mental eye that admits
from each thing, creature of
earth or sky or water, its own
effulgence, at whose source is
the single cell. Was the germinating
nucleus the icon of today? Look

49

on the mass of mountain, style,
shape, line, colour, yet look
inward to the core of being, self,
but look selflessly. See Spring come
again and again in the green shoots:
see the flush of Summer in the rose:
see the flame of the Fall from tree
casting its lavish hues, yet still see
nothing in unstilled time, but to still
the rushing tumble of nature in word
or stroke of brush – could he
who held the painter's knife or brush,
carry, transform that meaning
into the sentence or square
of canvas? Will the curtain of the mind
withdraw and transparency be his?
Look again in the iron bond of Winter
look to the bare bones of tree, of bush,
blasted, of barbed rose stems. Wait.
And the "house of being"* provides.
"Concealed gardeners" inhabit the trees,
he said. Blake named them "Angels"
as the silence of growth spoke to him.
Morning, noon and late, an old man
left the decent town of Aix.
Montagne Sainte Victoire, a presence
at a distance, did not disturb it,
but demanded him, Paul Cézanne,
to make the same sojourn through
ignorant streets. Insensate,
the populace howled at him. He,
who did not belong. This their daily
benediction at his setting out.
Children danced about him, sang,
hurled stones at him. He was
bound for the country where was

* 'house of being' Rilke: "words"

'l'atelier á Les Lauves.' Apples
strewed the floor, and would stay there.
They weighed as much in the mind
in paint as the hill. All belonged
to the one great whole, but on.
Cluttered, the way awkward, narrowing:
bush, tree, vegetable growth, ages old,
wide-spread, yield variants of green,
but mention of habitation, pink
roof-tops claim touches of attention
and beyond, the mountain's ever-changing
blue – but stones held the eye, the mind,
their differentiating thrust, counter
and spare, sometimes rust, sometimes
honey, reddening in the morning sun,
all known to him from life's beginning.
As boy he knew the challenge, the bruise
of bare boulder, limestone rock, grit
of sandstone, cuts in terrain, precipice
drops. He'd gone beyond Château Noir,
clambered up les Roches Barrées, then
as Sainte Victoire possessed his sight,
his first notation, first confrontation
on a sheet of white paper
that told what had not been done.
Now mind reached from the frail body
to contain all – the vertical pointing
stones, the horizontal wall of boulders.
To-fro the eye went, held, momentarily
within their bulk and firm outline.
All noted. To each and all, he,
the image-creator, maker, responds.
From any given form from earth, sky or water,
he could not turn away. Accept, he must.
To reject any is to reject all,
would imperil that state of grace
that granted him his innocent stroke.
Out of outcrops grew the Mountain.

A great line swept across the canvas
to the airy top. On this day sun shone,
revealed the muscled balks of stone
that ran athwart the hill, rebuffed
the eye, but mind took in
traverse and ascent to the top.
As by his own heart muscle, his being
committed to the blank rectangle
"the incarnation of the world."

Pen to paper: to Ambroise Vollard.
I work with dour determination,
will not give up. This day I caught
glimmerings of the Promised Land.
Will I, like the great Hebrew Chieftain,
never win to it? May I yet penetrate
its bounds? Why only now?
Why so late? I progress – but little.
Why so painfully? My art demands
pursuit of the single way, knowledge
of essential shapes written in nature.
Pen to paper: to Louis Arenches.
My realisation in art? – I think
I attain it more and more – with difficulty.
I have the strong experience of nature,
essential basis on which rests
the grandeur and beauty of all work to come.
Pen to paper: to Emile Bernard.
Forgive me. I repeat my telling you here.
You serve nature by the cylinder, sphere,
the cone, everything in the right perspective
so each side of object or plane directs
towards a central point. Lines parallel
to horizon stretch out, or to put it
quite another way, yields the spectacle.
Pater Omnipotens Aeterne Deus
displays before our eyes. Lines
perpendicular to the horizon give

profundity. Nature for us, humans,
is deeper than surface, so we must
introduce depth into our light
vibrations, reds and yellows and some blues
so we may feel the sensations of air.

Again the old man went his way – break fast,
studio, work, sustenance, sojourn
to the appointed place. The heat breathless.
"Earth, lay out my body. Rocks,
Crush my corpse!" I would cry out:
"O house of the dead, receive me living!"
Gone. Forty years, Cézanne, the poet,
gone. **Une Terrible Histoire**, "and the gap
between what is on the page and
what I feel then, feel now, the gap,
that which the brain tells, what
earth, stone-mountain, rock, sky,
tell, and this old hand would utter
on the page of canvas, yet there."
Still I pursue. Pursue for I am
pursued: seek for I am sought.
"My dear Paul, it is too hot, not
an air to breathe. Even so nature
presents itself to this painter
clearer than before, ever. It
spreads itself before my senses,
yet I cannot win its intensity,
cannot claim for brush and paint
that magnificence that works within
me." "My dear Paul, near four o'clock:
there is no air at all. The heat. Heat,
oppresses my brain. I cannot think.
I live in a void. Still I must paint."
He stares at Mountain and canvas,
canvas and mountain, the moment of
daring, of contact postponed, then
the beginning tortuous with darkest colour,

then layer upon layer, and spread
a little beyond, and then extending
the colours one atop the others, then
move to a new centre, and the same process,
but the centres run counter to each other,
even as in him counters meet, the engagement
a dialogue with self, but bred
of the sensation of the mountain,
weathered, worn, fulfilled in light and dark.
Contraries meet, dissension about him, in him,
and he goes to the mountain.
"Dear Paul, I continue my work
at 4.30 a.m. After 8 I cannot."
That day in the morning light
it spoke joyously to him.
Even the rocks bathed in sunlight.
Eyes and heart in that new air
lit every fold and convolution
of stony seam, boulder, cliff-face.
Trees, pine and olive, brightened
that day. "They wait for my brush.
The scene prepares itself for me,
will vanish. Perhaps I catch something.
Despite my weakness I am part of
this massive power, of this mass
that looks at me, has been there,
stays there, compels this veined hand.
Fearful, yet I am enlarged. I am
invaded by the energies of the mountain."
We look on the rectangle of canvas,
are part of what he has uncovered,
humbled, we receive an essence:
but no, he will not have it so.
"Dear Bernard, my cerebral disturbance,
so great, so confused, I am,
I fear for my frail reason". Doubts.
Still, will the unchanging provider
of the changing scene, shape, colour, line

allow him "to set down in my time, that
which tells the tale beyond telling
in words. Will the wilderness of stone
and hill speak to me again?" It is
late afternoon. Another tale is told.
Pitched, we are, into the wide scape,
thrust into, and beyond the pines,
farms, buildings roads, all transformed.
A weight of blocks of colour, but stabs,
demand attention. Given. But sense and
brain leap to the charge – the touch is lit –
Sainte Victoire – paint tells of tumult:
skies hurtle, burst with life-force.
This is cosmic talk. He is lifted up,
on a high: "I believe I am impenetrable."
He will return to Les Lauves. There
he looks no higher than flowers.
In the beam of his eye they offer
all hues – Spring, Summer, Autumn,
Winter. Earth substance, form of flower,
bulk of tree dismissed. He seeks,
gives us the moment of efflorescence.
It is a dialogue of colours. They talk
each to other, agree, disagree,
argue in silent conversation,
form a new union accepting difference.
Be silent with them. A sea of peace
holds him at the last touch of brush.
Monday, October 15 at Les Lauves,
a day of storm, thunder, skies
rent by lightning. He has walked.
An old man stands in the rain.
Hour upon hour it falls: will pass.
Skies will clear, and again
another dawn will break, colours
will flow in sky ways, green
to light-blue, for lark song.
It is a new awakening and he

there to transmit it, to transmute
the common miracle on a white sheet.
Two men find him all unknowing,
return him on their laundry cart,
home. The body is hard to lift
on to the bed. He is still. He sleeps.
Tuesday, October 16. At dawn
he goes down to the small garden
where in Summer he had begun
to paint Vallier, the gardener,
as he sat under the lime-tree,
white beard, straw hat on head,
half-asleep, he looked old. He'd
done him in oils, then a solid man.
Now in water-colours he shared
the transience of blossom on the bough.
The dialogue of brush with hill,
brush with earth's fruits, is ended.

When he painted a mountain
he painted an apple.
When he painted an apple
he painted a mountain.

Notes
Page 4, line 8: modified from Cézanne to Ambroise Vollard. 9 January 1903
Page 4, line 19: from Cézanne to Louis Arenches. 25 July 1904
Page 4, line 25: from Cézanne to Emile Bernard. 15 April 1904
Page 5, line 12: from the poem, *Une Terrible Histoire* by Cézanne
Page 5, line 21: from Cézanne to his son, Paul. 26 March 1906
Page 5, line 29: from Cézanne to his son, Paul. 14 August 1906
Page 6, line 34: from Cézanne to Emile Bernard. 21 September 1906
Page 7, line 16: from Cézanne to his son, Paul. 15 October 1906

The above excerpts from letters are from *Paul Cézanne Correspondance, recueillié,
annotée et prefacée par John Rewald.* Published Bernard Grasset, Paris 1978.

Velazquez

at the Edinburgh International Festival

For the begetter, Michael Clarke, of the Exhibition, *Velazquez in Seville* at the National Gallery of Scotland, August 1996.

He turned the searchlight of his mind
upon each and every object equally,
persons or things as if each in its
difference, might through the precision
of line and paint, each weighed in the
balance of a mind, would yield
final truth, each equally capable of
telling the tale that words
could not articulate, telling
in the silence of the canvas –
the egg, the water in the glass,
the gourd, the features of the old
woman, the boy, the seller of water,
water of life he sold – that
crystalline freshness was his
to sell, to sell that which was
beyond price –
O SANCTUS SANCTUS SANCTUS
he heard the silent talk of the
star, and it became humanity.

The references are to two paintings, *An Old Woman Cooking Eggs*, and *Water-seller of Seville*.

CREATURES

LOST

Black labrador retriever
answers to the name of Swimmer

Over the wall the leap was difficult,
awkward, more a scramble, managed
with the soft belly moulding to the stone.
Left by his master with a friend,
after much travel away from earth's smells,
from cabbage, rhubarb, decaying fungus at the gate,
leather, horse-dung, peat moor, whiff of gunshot,
brown burn, springy heather underfoot, from
sweet green grass, the wide strath, river, loch,
locked in a walled yard smelling of fish,
his kennel once a kiln for smoking haddock,
he barked till dark. At night the foghorn
boomed from the cliff. He howled back. Morning.
Down through the steep, twisting street he ran.
There was no doubting the way to the water.
'Fa echts ee?' speired Jeems the fisherman
baiting the great lines for his motor-boat:
'Thon's a richt blackie', as the dog hurried by,
slipping soft-footed over the moist pebbles,
then on with a bound to the launching pier,
and raced to a halt at the end. Gulls flew up
in a flurry about him. He sniffed the sea air.
It told tales unheard by him, but known
from his unknown past in traces of the brain,
buried memories waiting on the place, time,
the event, for transmission to nerves, to muscle, to act.
The acts in Labrador were for survival. In winter
the ground is iron. Along the irregular
coast-line, serrated skerries, towering cliffs
threatened the small craft of the fishermen,
colonists of the indented bays. In summer cod
and haddock soused in brine, hung on frames
in the open air to dry to be held for winter.
Survival required co-operation. To the North
Eskimos made huskies their agents for transport.

Fishermen on the Atlantic's face found allies
in dogs, strong and sinuous swimmers,
accurate, gentle-mouthed they took back
to the boats, cod and haddock, even sea-trout
unmarked, through the wash and buffet of water.
They took the name of their place abroad – Labrador.
A boy with all the force he could, from the pier,
threw a stick out to sea. "Get it! Go! Get it!"
Dog launched himself. The swell was slow, easy.
He was part of the heaving mass, yielding to it,
it yielding to him, salt sea lifted him up, buoyant.
Once, long time back, a child, girl, Morag,
slipped from the river bank to the Spey.
In a moment he was at her, held her clothes,
bunched, face above water, just, with difficulty,
pushed hard against the stream to outstretched hands.
'Swimmer,' she called him. So baptised the name stuck.
The stick offered itself to his jaws. But deep beneath,
over the rocky sea-floor a shadow, a swift shape
that carried a command. Here was fish.
The stick floated free. He dived.
In Labrador the sea men knew the flow
and drag of currents, the force of seas
in narrow rents the boats must risk
to win the open sea, knew when to, when
not to, crew boats, men and dogs to hunt.
Boys on the shores of Scottish waters dive
into the breaking wave, giving their bodies
to the undertow, hold breath till sudden
the dynamic fails. Freed they burst surface
into generous air. They know where force
is spent, know too that the calm surface far out
does not disclose below the penetrating race that
holds and brings all caught to the blind depths.
From the pier he saw dog seize the stick,
saw it float free. No more.

Speired the man: "Fa echts ee?" "Nae man has me,
but the shavie watters o the cauld North Sea".

61

Koala

At Cleland National Park, South Australia

I

Very slowly he moved with sleep
in his drink-sodden eyes
about the trunk. His position
of backside to me, perhaps,
was not intended as insult,
but not, not a camera shot.

Position reversed – cradled
between tree-arm and trunk,
he is looking at me,
so I flatter myself till
I observe the eyes are closed.

Still the relaxed poise suggests,
or allows for, the acceptance
of another's presence,
or was he just bored
with the whole human race?

II

Without a "by your leave" or "may I",
the guide/presenter of the show
plants the creature on my chest.
The tourists click their cameras,
and "Doesn't he love the dear old man!"

No hint of love or hate, but
indifferently the mammal's claws
are penetrating to my skin.
Am I being signalled that
he and his kin belong
with the dark people
who did not welcome our coming?

Rebuke

There was bread left over
at breakfast, a heel of brown bread,
and I broke it and put it on the stone
ledge at the window: and sparrows came,
a blackbird and a black-capped tit,
and it all went quickly.

And the next morning I did the same,
and it went quickly. Then
the bitter wind came and I kept
the window tight-shut, and a sparrow,
one sparrow, sat on a bush by the window
and cursed me in cheeps. So

I put out more bread, and its friends came
and munched and munched and munched,
and the next day the wind blew colder,
and I kept shut the window;
and the cheeping and cheepering went on.
Why should I fear a sparrow's rebuke
when Sarajevo weeps its eyes out?

Repentance

Now I am making a brown parcel
of all my tomorrows, each one a song,
(but of how many I do not know)
to put on the ledge for the cheeping sparrows.

I could guess them, yet still would not know
how to deal with my stained futures.
Sparrows know how to treat
each moment of the day.

In the peek of an eye,
in the flirt of a wing,
in the peck of a beak
in the dust – they know
a meal from a mote.

Haiku Envoi

The sea trembles – voiceless.
It is the rare moment
when a word is sought.

Notes

On the Edge – The Broch *p. 4*
    1. *The Broch* – local name for Fraserburgh
    2. There were several James Buchans in Mid Street, Inverallochy, hence the substitution of numbers for the name. Gilbert, his son, also came to be known as 7½.
    3. The sight of Mormond Hill from the sea, from a particular angle gave the skipper the assurance he would get a good run in to Fraserburgh Harbour.
    4. Two reproductions, one of a horse, the other of a deer, were laid out in white stone on Mormond Hill. They were not ancient but Victorian.
    5. 'immemorial' of course. The boy got it wrong, or there was a syllable too many for the rhythms.
    6. In February 1993 I was invited by George Gunn, then Writer-in-Residence in Macduff for Banff and Buchan, to present a selection of my poems, and to write a new one for the first of *The Five Touns Festivals*, which was held in Fraserburgh, my home town. The programme was also sustained by Edwin Morgan. Since the poem was to be performed before a local audience, the episodes and references had to be factually correct, as they are, though there is some exaggeration in my reporting. On leaving my home at 2 Victoria Street, the milk cart became airborne, at least it felt like that. I have to admit too that my grandfather was not present on the occasion, but he did in his nineties, greet all, his walking stick raised, with "Praise the Lord!"
    7. James Buchan spoke these words in conversation for the Scottish Home Service of the BBC.

Ian in the Broch *p. 18*
    Having visited Scotland's Lighthouse Museum, Ian McNab and I climbed the steps of Kinnaird Head lighthouse to look at the light at close quarters. Once set in motion the three ton light could be moved by the pressure of a finger. I quoted from my poem *Castle Turned Lighthouse* (Collected Poems) written in 1943, "Ballbearing, frictionless lamp." Ian McNab pointed out they were not ballbearings. They were "tapered rollers." This set the poem going. I had met the whole man, engineer, singer, Brocher.

Invocation *p. 21*
    1. The occasion was the annual party of the Scottish Poetry Library. The Director, Tessa Ransford, had published *Medusa*, a collection of her poems. The Flat is above the library which contains the works of poets, past and present. Not far from the library in the High Street, had been Sibbald's Library and following it, Ramsay's Library.

Epistle 1: To Edwin Morgan *p. 22*
    Edwin Morgan and Carl MacDougall invited me to contribute a poem to *New Writing, Scotland*. I had just returned from the United States, where at St. Andrews College, North Carolina, I met Ezra Pound's daughter Mary de Rachewiltz. She

was curator of his manuscripts at Yale. She was annotating *The Cantos*. She thanked me for information about Joseph MacLeod. I told her how he persuaded Eliot to publish MacLeod's first collection of poems, *The Ecliptic*, in 1928. To bring to mind something of the Pound 'atmosphere' I allowed into my letter 'cd' for could, and 'shd' for should.

Epistle 5: A Thank-You To John Bellany *p. 27*
The three figures of fishermen have a religious implication. In his *Introduction* to the catalogue for the 1986 Exhibition of Paintings, Water-colours and Drawings at the Scottish National Gallery of Modern Art, Keith Hartley wrote:
"But Bellany held tight to his convictions and was not afraid to tackle even the most traditional of subjects: the Crucifixion."
Yet the subject matter is far removed from the accepted iconography of classical paintings.
"In *Allegory (1964)* he established a basic approach to the raw material of his own experiences... The three gutted fish, nailed up to dry on their posts ... are an allegory of the Crucifixion and of all the cruelty, suffering and sacrifice that that event symbolised."
This is, as Keith Hartley described, part of a "monumental scheme." The three fishermen, shabby, cast down, but with grim determination in their features is realistic yet evidently reveals that religious interpretation of life accepted by those who hunted the fish.

At Mayakovsky's Statue *p. 31*
Mayakovsky an idealist communist turned against the Soviet bureaucracy. Frustrated, he committed suicide. I visited the statue which was bronze, not stone, but the stone image suited my purpose.

The Crescent *p. 33*
1. Number 33, the end house. Martin Prestige was married to Lucina.

Elizabeth in the Garden *p. 34*
1. The windflower plant was given to my wife by William Gillies from his garden at Temple village in the late 1960s. Apparently, by the 1980s I had forgotten its name. I attempted and failed to write the poem apart from the first lines, mislaid them and found them about 1995, the year after my wife's death.

Weys of Self-Preservin Natur *p. 42*
1. *Sweet Thames*. Edmund Spenser.
2. *The City of London*. William Dunbar
3. *The New Testament in Scots*. W. L. Lorimer (1983)

The Chair *p. 45*
The drawing was for the cover of *Interim* (University of Nevada Press) by Loucinda Wilder Stevens. Quotations used and adapted from Van Gogh's letters to his brother Theo.

GLOSSARY

a all
aa everybody
afore before
ablow below
a'body everybody
aboot about
agen again
ahint behind
aifter after
aince once
airches arches
an lat thae and allow those
aneath beneath
anither another
atween between
auld old
aye always
ayont beyond
ba game ball game
bairn child
bairnie little child
baith both
beryall jewel, jewel-like
bi by
bit but
blackie black dog
blaw blow
bleat complain
blin blind
blint blinded
blootered booted
bodie body, human being
bondit bonded
braid broad
braith breath
braw fine
breist breast
brig, brigge bridge
Broch local name for Fraserburgh
Broch loon Fraserburgh boy
brocht brought
buik book

cairry carry
cam came
cauld cold
chiel fellow
chievin achieving
chine, chyne chain
claes clothes
close passageway (gen. to a tenement)
coorse rough
crood crowd
cud could
dae do
daith death
deaved deafened
deef deaf
deein dying
deid dead
derk dark
dooncome downfall
doon-takin humiliation
doot doubt
doun down
doups buttocks
duin wioot done without
echts owns
ee eye
een eyes
e'en even
eeseless useless
eidently diligent
eneuch enough
fae, frae from
faain falling
faither father
faur eence where once
feart afraid
feenished finished
fit foot
fit's deein? what's doing?
fit wye? what way?
flasht flashed
flim-flam-fleerie flimsy, superficial

fou's aa? how's everybody?
gaed went
gaithered gathered
gan gyte gone crazy
gang go
gawpt gaped
geck stare
gied given
gien given
girn complain
gowden golden
graip an iron pronged fork
grander a grand person
greetin weeping
grippit gripped
gryte great
gryte herted great hearted
guid-wife wife
gweed good
hail whole
hame home
hantle a fair number
haud hold
hauden holding, huddling
haun hand
heich high
heid head
heid o 't head of it
heilan deems highland women
heist hoist
hert heart
hertit hearted
hid had
hine awa far away
his us
his loons us boys
hisna has not
hoo how
ile an saut oil and salt
ill teenit ill tempered
ingaun ingoing
ither other
ithers others
jile jail

jined joined
jist just
keek look, peep
ken know
kenna know not
kenspeckle show-off,
                conspicuous
kent knew
kittled tickled
lang long
lealty loyalty
leeds languages
licht light
lichtly lightly
lichtnin lightening
look awa look away
loons boys
loupin leaping
ludgins lodgings
lugs ears
ma my
mair more
maist most
mannie man
mart market
maun must
meen moon
merchantis merchants
meth might
mindin remembering
mither mother
mixter-maxter mixed up
monkey made a fool of
mou mouth
mows joke
mune moon
ony only
oor our
oot out
oot-bye outside, nearby
oot o' sicht out of sight
oot, stracht straight ahead
owre over
partan edible crab

pechin breathing heavily
peep low light
peerie small
Peterheid Peterhead
peyed payed
pints points
pit it put it
pit-oot put out
plooed ploughed
pooer power
preclare very clear,
              illustrious
preen-heid pin head
pylers pillars
quaet quiet
quines lasses, girls
raxed reached
retour return
richt right
rin-in run in
risin rising
ryvers rivers
sae so
saft soft
safticks greenback crabs
           used for bait
sair sore
sangs songs
sanle sand eels
saut salt
saxty sixty
scartit scratched
scrawled crawled
sel self
sgriobh write (Gael.)
shall shell
sheenan shining
shaucle shanty
shavie deceitful
sic such
sic a girnan such a
             complaining
sicht sight
siller silver

skraiches screeches
slipt, slippit slipped
sma-boukit small built
sma glen small valley
smore a smother every-
                thing
snash insult, impudence
socht sought
sog soaked or wet place
soom swim
sooth south
soun sound
spewed vomited
squeel school
stane stone
stap stop
staun stand
steamy wash-house
steen stone
steen wa stone wall
stracht straight
stravaig wander
swanne swan
swymme swin
syne then
tae to
tak tent give heed
taigelt tangled
tap top
tatties potatoes
teemed emptied
teuchats lapwing
thegither together
thochts thoughts
thon yon, that
thrawn obstinate
threided threaded
thunner thunder
ticht tight
till until
til't a' richt into it all right
tither the other
toun town
trimmlin trembling

twa two
unkennan unknowing
unnerstan understand
vennels narrow lane
          between houses
vrocht worked hard
wa wall
wanchancy treacherous
warlds worlds
Warld's End Edinburgh
          vennel
wark work
watter water
wecht weight
weel well
weemen women

weyes ways
wha who
wha's who is this?
whaur where
wi freens with friends
wioot without
wir ours
wis we
wites waits
witin waiting
wrack seaweed
wrang wey wrong way
wurd word
wyngis wings
yammering talking
          incoherently

yelloch yell, scream
yestreen yesterday

hid the deid-chack knockit
had the death watch beetle
knocked

Puddlestinker a person
who lived in Hanover
Street, Fraserburgh, known
many years ago as
Puddlestink, on account of
its slummy appearance